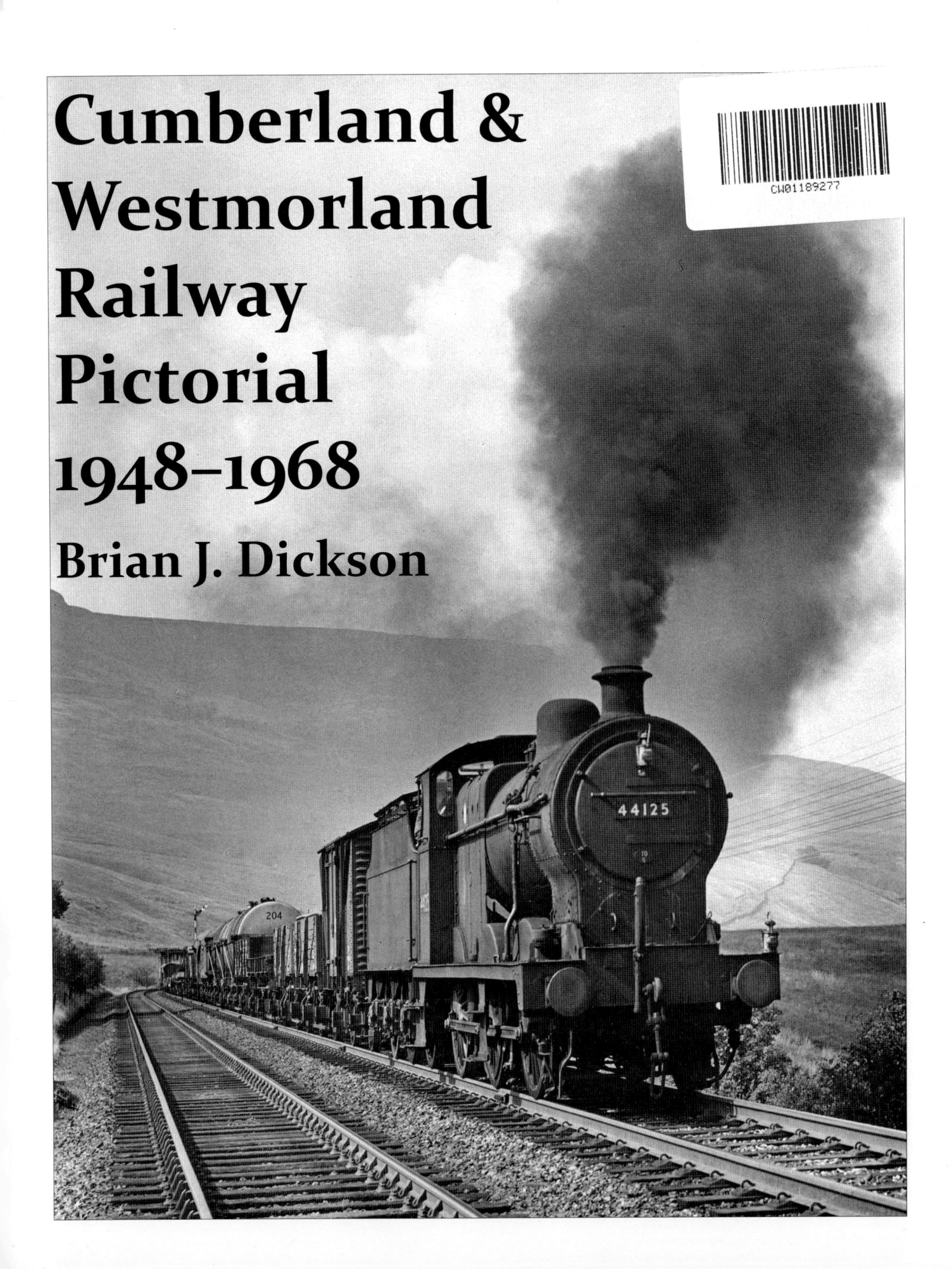

Cumberland & Westmorland Railway Pictorial 1948–1968

Brian J. Dickson

©Kestrel Railway Books and Brian J. Dickson 2014

Kestrel Railway Books
PO Box 269
SOUTHAMPTON
SO30 4XR

www.kestrelrailwaybooks.co.uk

ISBN 978-1-905505-32-6

All rights reserved. No part of this publication may be reproduced, stored in a retrieval system, transmitted in any form or by any means, electronic, mechanical, or photocopied, recorded or otherwise, without the consent of the publisher in writing.

Every effort has been made to trace copyright holders of the photographs reproduced. Apologies are offered to any who may have been missed.

Printed by The Amadeus Press

Front cover: It is mid-afternoon on Saturday 30th April 1966, and the calm of Mallerstang Common, in the valley of the river Eden, is being broken by the approach of a hard working Black 5 nearing the summit of the climb to Ais Gill. At the head of a southbound goods train from Carlisle, long-term Kingmoor resident No 44902 is captured crossing Ais Gill viaduct with the now demolished "Hangman's Bridge" seen near the rear of the train. Through the haze, Wild Boar Fell in the background looks more welcoming than its reputed character. *(Martin Welch)*

Back cover, top: Saturday 16th June 1962. Highlighted by the mid-afternoon sunshine at Shap Wells, ex-LMS class 4 2-6-4 tank No 42424 gives rear end assistance for the 5½-mile climb to the summit at Shap to a 13-coach Manchester to Glasgow train that is hauled by BR Standard class 7 4-6-2 No 70023 *Venus*. The driver of the Britannia was possibly being over-cautious in judging the locomotive's abilities to handle a load of approximately 450 tons, unassisted on the 1 in 75 gradient. *(NA Machell)*

Back cover, bottom: Skirting the site of the ex-Caledonian Viaduct goods yard at Carlisle, a Derby Lightweight DMU has just left Citadel station with an early evening Carlisle to Silloth train on Saturday 13th June 1964. Introduced during November 1954 to replace the steam-hauled stock on the Silloth branch, they continued running this service until the branch was closed to passenger traffic in September 1964. *(NA Machell)*

Title Page: May 1963. This impressive photograph portrays hardworking ex-LMS class 4F 0-6-0 No 44125 as it approaches Ais Gill summit with the 1.04pm goods train from Carlisle to Skipton. This Fowler designed class was introduced in 1924 with this particular locomotive being built at Crewe works in 1925; she managed to survive 40 years to be withdrawn during 1965. In the background are seen the desolate slopes of Wild Boar Fell. *(Peter J Robinson)*

Below: Friday 25th May 1951. Seen here in charge of the up Royal Scot near Wreay, just south of Carlisle, are the two LMS-designed diesel electric locomotives 10000 and 10001. Hauling the train, which consists entirely of the then new Mark 1 coaches, 10000 still bears its LMS origin on the bodyside. Built at Derby works toward the end of 1947, she would finally be withdrawn late in 1963. Her sister 10001 was also built at Derby, entering service in 1948; she would finally be withdrawn in 1966. *(R Hewitt)*

Introduction

The stunning scenery of the Cumberland and Westmorland Fells belies the nature of the railway routes that cut their way through to the north. The long climb on the Settle and Carlisle line in both directions to Ais Gill summit at 1169 feet, takes place through some of the wildest and bleakest landscape in the country. Commencing in the valley of the River Ribble at Settle Junction, it proceeds between Ingleborough and Pen-y-Ghent with a 16-mile climb, much of it at 1 in 100 gradients to Blea Moor and thence to Ais Gill before skirting Wild Boar Fell and reaching Kirkby Stephen and Appleby. It then follows the valley of the River Eden running through the rich farming countryside to reach Carlisle.

In comparison, the West Coast Main Line (WCML) basically climbs continuously for about 33 miles from just above sea level at Carnforth, north through Oxenholme and Tebay to reach the testing 5½-mile, 1 in 75, ascent to Shap summit at 916 feet. There follows a gentle run, again through rich farming country, into Carlisle following the valley of the River Petteril.

The most scenic of the lines running through Cumberland was undoubtedly the 39 miles of the former Cockermouth, Keswick and Penrith Railway that traversed the highly productive farming country between Penrith and Cockermouth. Whilst having the imposing bulks of both Saddleback and Skiddaw as a backdrop near Keswick, it also skirted the beautiful Bassenthwaite Lake before arriving at the imposing station at Cockermouth. Initially established to facilitate the movement east of haematite ore from west Cumberland to the iron works in County Durham, this route also saw huge amounts of coke travelling west from the ovens in County Durham to the iron works in west Cumberland.

Many of the photographs chosen for this volume reflect the remote nature of railway operation through these fells, and are a lasting tribute to the many photographers who braved the sometimes wild conditions in their pursuit of that special shot.

The period from January 1948 until August 1968, just over 20 years in duration, saw many changes to railway operations in the counties of Cumberland, Westmorland and the North Lonsdale district of Lancashire – collectively now known as Cumbria. Nationalisation of the railways brought a feeling of renewal within the management and workforce of the railways, especially, after the dark days of the Second World War, and as larger sums of money were allocated to the railways, track maintenance and quality improved allowing higher running speeds and consequently shorter journey times between city centres.

The new London Midland Region within British Railways was already well equipped with many modern steam locomotive classes, Sir William Stanier being central to their design and construction. Such classes as the Princess Coronation and Princess Royal were the hardworking backbone of the WCML express passenger services, and his mixed-traffic Black 5 and 3-cylinder Jubilee locomotives were strong and efficient workhorses over all the old LMS territory. Earlier classes, such as the Fowler designed 3-cylinder Patriots and Royal Scots that had been central to LMS passenger services before Stanier joined the company, were still performing good work throughout the region.

In the north-west area of England covered by this book, the pre-grouping classes of locomotives became a rarer sight after Nationalisation, with only about 60 examples remaining allocated to the depots at Barrow, Carnforth, Carlisle Upperby, Penrith and Workington. These pre-grouping locomotives were to be seen mostly around Barrow where the ex-Furness Railway 0-6-0s were based, Carnforth where some ex-LNWR 0-8-0s were based for heavy goods traffic and Penrith, Workington and Carlisle, where a few ex-LNWR "Cauliflower" 0-6-0s operated the services on the former Cockermouth, Keswick and Penrith Railway route. Otherwise, LMS-built classes were prominent with many class 4, 2-6-4 tanks, Black 5s and the Moguls designed by both Hughes and Ivatt being seen on operations throughout the area.

Construction of several ex-LMS classes continued into the early 1950s with the final examples of the Fairburn 2-6-4 4MT tanks and Stanier Black 5s appearing in 1951, the last of Ivatt's 2-6-0 4MTs rolling out of Doncaster works in 1952 and the remaining examples of his 2-6-0 2MTs coming into traffic as late as March 1953 from Swindon works.

The first of BR's new Standard steam locomotive types appeared in January 1951, when amid much publicity No 70000 *Britannia* was rolled out of Crewe works. Road testing took place during that month between Crewe and Carlisle, and the locomotive was named at a ceremony in Marylebone station on 31st January of that year. Unlike the rest of the LMR, depots in the North West of England did not initially receive any of the new Standard locomotives, Carlisle Kingmoor being the only recipient in 1952 when the last five Clans were sent there, Nos 72005–72009 spending their entire short working lives allocated to that depot.

In December 1954, the British Transport Commission published its plan for the "Modernisation and Re-equipment of British Railways". In locomotive terms this predicted the end of steam power by announcing that no new steam locomotives would be built after the end of the 1956 programme. A pilot scheme was devised whereby 174 main-line diesel locomotives would be purchased from various manufacturers, and then subjected to rigorous testing before further orders were placed. In all, 160 of these locomotives would be built with electric transmission, and they would range from an 800hp Type A (later Type 1) for goods work to a 2,300hp Type C (later Type 4) for express passenger trains. In practice, many orders were placed for large numbers of locomotives without any prolonged testing, with the result that some designs with inherent problems were produced and consequently had short working lives.

Prior to the introduction of the main line diesel locomotives envisaged by British Railways in the 1954 Modernisation Report, the LMS were instrumental in producing and rigorously testing the diesel electric form of traction. H.G. Ivatt was the driving force behind the experiment that had begun in 1946 to produce two locomotives at Derby works to be fitted with English Electric engines and generators. The first locomotive, No 10000, entered traffic in December 1947, proudly bearing the LMS initials on its bodywork; the second locomotive, No 10001, followed in July 1948 bearing no sign of its LMS origins. After a lengthy testing period the two locomotives were seen from 1949 onward regularly hauling the "Royal Scot" service between London and Glasgow. Generally acknowledged as the precursors to the highly successful English Electric Type 4s, which appeared during 1959, they were withdrawn in 1963 and 1966 respectively.

Towards the end of 1948, the Railway Executive had

formed a committee to compare the relative merits of steam, diesel and electric motive power. This committee did not report until 1951, and in the meantime a working party was formed to evaluate the use of lightweight diesel trains. The conclusion of the investigation was outlined in yet another report in March 1952, which led to the introduction of these lightweight diesel trains known as diesel multiple units (DMUs).

While work on building DMUs and main line diesel locomotives was progressing, steam traction still reigned supreme with services on the WCML being powered by Princess Coronation, Princess Royal and Britannia Pacific locomotives based in Glasgow, Crewe and London. Inter-city passenger traffic working through the North West was in the capable hands of the 3-cylinder Jubilee, Royal Scot and Patriot locomotives shared with Black 5s. Local traffic tended to be handled by both Black 5s and the many 4MT 2-6-4 tanks allocated to depots in the area. Branch-line goods traffic that was initially handled by the ageing pre-grouping 0-6-0s was quickly taken over by Ivatt designed Moguls. Heavier goods services were handled by Black 5 and "Crab" locomotives with the occasional ex-LNWR 0-8-0 being seen, and Stanier designed class 8F 2-8-0s very often working through goods trains between Scotland and the South.

The Midland Railway had been forward thinking enough to electrify the Lancaster, Morecambe and Heysham services using an overhead 6600V, 25-cycle, AC system during 1908. This service continued until 1951, when the equipment was judged to be life-expired, and was replaced by push/pull steam trains. From August 1953, the electric service was re-commenced using ex-LNWR Willesden Junction to Earls Court stock that had been converted to run on the overhead system using the 25kV, 50-cycle, AC system that became standard for the WCML electrification scheme. During January 1966, this system was finally abandoned and the services taken over by DMUs.

The first DMUs to be produced under the British Railways plan of 1952 were designed and manufactured at Derby works during 1954, and entered traffic between Leeds and Bradford in June of that year. These generally became referred to as Derby Lightweight units, with the second batch to be built during 1954 being sent to Carlisle to operate in the Cumberland area. Services commenced in November 1954 between Carlisle and Silloth, in January 1955 between Carlisle, Penrith, Keswick and Workington and in February 1955 between Carlisle, Maryport, Workington and Whitehaven. These introductions did of course result in many examples of pre-grouping locomotives such as the ex-LNWR "Cauliflower" locomotives, used on the Workington, Cockermouth, Keswick and Penrith route, being made redundant and sent for scrap.

As these DMUs settled down to give a new clean service for passengers, local goods and through passenger services remained in the hands of Ivatt Moguls, Black 5s and 4MT 2-6-4 tanks. Express passenger trains on the WCML and the Settle and Carlisle routes were still being hauled by Princess Royal, Princess Coronation, Royal Scot, Patriot and Jubilee locomotives, with an increasing number of the new Britannia class Standards also seeing use on these routes.

June 1957 saw delivery of the first of the Pilot Scheme main line diesel locomotives with English Electric Type 1 diesel electric No D8000 which, after initial testing, was sent to depots around the UK for evaluation, which included trials on the WCML into Carlisle. The first batch of 20 locomotives of this type were in service by the Spring of 1958, closely followed in the middle of the same year by the Metropolitan-Vickers Co-Bo Type 2, which after evaluation were used on the Condor overnight goods service between Hendon and Glasgow introduced in March 1959.

It was also in the Spring of 1959 that the first of the successful English Electric Type 4s were delivered to the LMR depots at Camden, Crewe, Liverpool and Manchester. Having proved themselves to be reliable locomotives in service with the Eastern Region, they were immediately put into service hauling express passenger traffic on the WCML, and by September of that year were regularly working the Royal Scot.

In the North West during the early 1960s, the dieselisation of services slowly gathered momentum with an increasing number of through passenger trains being diesel hauled. On the other hand, goods services remained the stronghold of steam power with Stanier designed Black 5 and 8F locomotives being prominent. With the increased use of diesel traction in the Eastern Region, a number of the displaced Britannia class locomotives were allocated to Carnforth and Carlisle depots, where they were employed on the WCML.

On 27th March 1963, the Beeching Report on "The Reshaping of British Railways" was published, and it made devastating reading for passengers, employees and enthusiasts as it proposed the closure of many branch lines and the removal of many stopping services, leading to closure of about one-third of the network and the loss of approximately 70,000 jobs in the industry. Services in Cumberland and Westmorland would not escape the "axe". The complete closure of the Settle and Carlisle route, Barrow to Whitehaven, the former CK&PR route, the Silloth branch, Ulverston to Lakeside and Carnforth to Wennington were planned, and the cessation of all stopping services between Lancaster and Carlisle would leave the bulk of Cumberland and Westmorland without any passenger services. Fortunately, not all the Beeching recommendations were acted upon and the Cumbrian Coast line survived, as did the Settle and Carlisle route.

By the mid-1960s whilst other regions saw the quickening pace in the dieselization of services, the depots in the north-west of England still retained much of their allocation of steam locomotives, indeed Carnforth shed and the countryside stretching north to Tebay, Shap and Carlisle became a huge draw for enthusiasts wishing to soak up the atmosphere during those last few years of steam operation on British Railways.

By the end of 1962, the last of the Princess Royal class had been withdrawn from service and October 1964 saw the complete withdrawal of the remaining Princess Coronation locomotives. 1962 also saw the introduction of one of the most successful types of diesel electric locomotives to be bought by British Railways – the Brush-built Type 4s. A total of 512 examples were constructed over a five-year period, and they proved so reliable that some examples are still to be found today being used by main-line operators.

So it was that Cumberland and Westmorland would see the final operations connected with British Railways main-line steam locomotives on Sunday 11th August 1968. The "Fifteen Guinea Special" departed Liverpool Lime Street at 9.10am prompt for Manchester Victoria behind Black 5 No 45110. The Manchester to Blackburn and Carlisle section was hauled by Britannia No 70013 *Oliver Cromwell* with the return to Manchester via Ais Gill behind Black 5 Nos 44871 and 44781. The final return leg from Manchester to Liverpool was handled by 45110 again. This final journey was accompanied by thousands of spectators lining station platforms and vantage points along the route wishing to have a glimpse of this momentous occasion.

April 1948. Still bearing its LMS identity, ex-LNWR 18in goods class (or "Cauliflower") 0-6-0 No 28589 stands quietly beside the water tower at Keswick while taking water. One of a class of over 300 examples designed by FW Webb, and introduced in 1880, she was built at Crewe works in 1901, and survived a further four years to be withdrawn numbered 58421 late in 1952. *(RF Roberts, SLS)*

Wednesday 10th August 1949. Sporting its new British Railways number and identity along with a 21A (Saltley) shed code, ex-LMS class 5 4-6-0 No 45268 makes easy work of its approach to Ais Gill summit with a five-coach up express. Built by Armstrong Whitworth as one of the earlier examples of the class in 1936, she would be withdrawn at the end of main line steam use in the UK in August 1968, having served 32 years. *(H Weston)*

May 1950. Ex-LNWR class G 0-8-0 No 49134 is seen here approaching Oxenholme with a goods train from the Windermere branch. Constructed at Crewe works in 1910 during the Bowen-Cooke period, the design was originally introduced in 1892 by FW Webb. Over 500 examples were built, and many were subsequently rebuilt over a long period. This example of these sturdy hard working locomotives survived until 1962 before being withdrawn. *(RF Roberts, SLS)*

May 1950. Bearing its new British Railways number, but with its previous ownership still faintly visible on the tender, ex-LNWR "Cauliflower" 0-6-0 No 58396 moves smartly away from Keswick station with a Cockermouth to Penrith passenger train. Allocated to Workington depot (12D), this example of the class was built at Crewe works in 1900 and was withdrawn in 1953. A further example of the class can be seen in the background. *(P Ransome-Wallis)*

May 1950. The LMS mixed traffic workhorse was the Black 5 locomotive designed by Sir William Stanier and introduced to traffic during 1934. A total of 842 examples were constructed by various railway works and independent manufacturers with the last of the class appearing in 1951. The example shown here is No 45414, seen working a down goods near Oxenholme. Constructed by Armstrong Whitworth in 1937, she would be withdrawn during 1965. *(RF Roberts, SLS)*

May 1950. Preparing to leave Carlisle station with the 4.55pm two-coach train to Penrith, "Cauliflower" No 58396 is blowing off vigorously whilst waiting for the right of way. A long-time resident of Workington depot, she was one of eight locomotives of the class allocated to depots in Cumberland and used on the passenger and goods traffic over the branches in that county. *(RF Roberts, SLS)*

May 1950. With a fourteen coach load behind the tender, ex-LMS class 8P Princess Coronation 4-6-2 No 46223 *Princess Alice* is seen approaching Oxenholme with the up Mid-Day Scot. Built at Crewe works in 1937, this locomotive was originally clad in a streamline casing which was removed prior to Nationalisation. Allocated to Polmadie depot in Glasgow, she would be withdrawn from service during 1963. Note the Windermere branch swinging away north on the left of the photograph. *(RF Roberts, SLS)*

Monday 5th June 1950. Showing the correct lamp code for a "stopper"', class 2 2-6-0 No 46449 moves smartly away from Penrith with the 1.25pm three-coach passenger train for Workington. This almost 40-mile journey was timetabled to take 1hr 22min, and would traverse the beautifully situated route of the former Cockermouth, Keswick and Penrith Railway, opened in 1865. The locomotive is only three months old, having been constructed at Crewe works in March 1950. She would only survive 17 years to be withdrawn in 1967. *(ED Bruton)*

Monday 5th June 1950. Super-power at the head of an express goods train. The 1.55pm Carlisle to Edge Hill is seen approaching Penrith behind ex-LMS class 8F 2-8-0 No 48289 piloting ex-LMS class 5, 4-6-0 No 45412. The 8F had an interesting history. Being constructed as part of a Ministry of Supply order by Beyer, Peacock & Co in 1940, she was numbered 413 (later 70413) by the War Department, and transferred to the Iranian State Railway system in 1941. She appears to have been returned to the UK in 1948, and was purchased by British Railways in 1949. She would be withdrawn in 1966. The Black 5 had been built by Armstrong Whitworth in 1937, and would be withdrawn after 30 years' service in 1967. *(ED Bruton)*

Monday 7th August 1950. Only four months old and looking very smart in black lined livery is class 2 2-6-0 No 46455. Built at Crewe works, she would be withdrawn during 1967, but is seen here passing Cockermouth South signalbox working a bank holiday special from Workington to Keswick. *(PB Whitehouse)*

August 1950. Seen near Troutbeck on the former Cockermouth, Keswick and Penrith Railway route is ex-LNWR "Cauliflower" 0-6-0 No 58396 working the 11.50am Workington to Penrith passenger train which includes a four-wheeled van. Note the change in size of the cab-side numbers when compared to the photographs on page 6 taken in May of the same year. *(PB Whitehouse)*

Saturday 5th August 1950. No 58396 is seen again, this time leaving Penruddock station with the 4.53pm Penrith to Workington train. The passenger services on this beautiful cross-country route survived in a truncated form until final closure in March 1972. *(Millbrook House Ltd)*

Wednesday 13th June 1951. An unusual study of the effect of superelevation with class 4 2-6-4 tank No 42573 taking water on the up main at Penrith whilst the fireman controls the flow. The locomotive based at Carnforth depot (11A) is in charge of the 1.51pm Carlisle to Oxenholme "stopper". One of the Stanier designed variants of this successful class, she was constructed by the NBL in 1936, and would be withdrawn late in 1964.
(W Philip Conolly)

August 1951. Working hard with a Glasgow-bound express, ex-LMS class 4 2-6-4 tank No 42314 is piloting ex-LMS class 8P Princess Coronation 4-6-2 No 46240 *City of Coventry* as they approach the summit at Shap. 42314, bearing the early British Railways lettering, was one of the successful parallel-boilered Fowler designed tanks introduced in 1927. Built at Derby works in 1928, she would be withdrawn in 1962. *City of Coventry* was constructed at Crewe works in 1940 as a streamlined example of the class. Losing the streamlined casing prior to Nationalisation, she would not be withdrawn until two years after the tank locomotive in 1964. *(G Clarke)*

August 1951. An early example of the original Fowler designed class 4 2-6-4 tank is seen here at Lancaster Castle station. The fireman on No 42301 appears to have things well in hand prior to departure with a local train. Constructed at Derby works in 1927, she would be withdrawn in 1963. *(Eric Treacy, NRM)*

Wednesday 1st August 1951. In bright evening sunshine, ex-LMS class 4 2-6-4 tank No 42544 of Carnforth depot, is working the 5.00pm Oxenholme to Carlisle local, which appears to consist mostly of ex-LNER coaching stock. Seen here in the open countryside near Scout Green on the climb to Shap summit, she was one of the Stanier variants of this class. Built at Derby works in 1935, she would survive until 1962 before being withdrawn. *(JD Mills)*

Saturday 24th May 1952. Only three months into her short life, Standard class 6P5F Clan 4-6-2 No 72004 *Clan Macdonald* makes a spirited start away from Lancaster Castle station past the impressive No 4 box with the 9.43am Liverpool Exchange to Glasgow Central express. Constructed at Crewe works in February of the same year, she would be allocated to Polmadie in Glasgow for her entire working life, which only lasted until 1962. After withdrawal she lay stored for a further two years at Polmadie before going for scrap in 1964. The Clans were originally designed as a lighter version of the Britannia class, destined for work on the ex-Highland main line between Perth and Inverness, but instead were primarily used on the WCML between Glasgow, Carlisle, Liverpool and Manchester. *(ED Bruton)*

Monday 26th May 1952. Ex-LMS class 3 2-6-2 tank No 40064 is drifting down Shap near Scout Green with a short goods train from Penrith to Tebay. This (surprisingly) relatively unsuccessful Fowler designed class of tanks, introduced in 1930, followed the success of his 2-6-4 tanks introduced in 1927. Constructed at Derby works in 1932, this example would be withdrawn in 1961. *(ED Bruton)*

Wednesday 4th June 1952. Working north through the wooded countryside near Oxenholme with a train of empty coke wagons from Millom Iron Works, near Barrow, to Derwenthaugh in the North Eastern Region near Newcastle is ex-LMS class 4F 0-6-0 No 44292. The locomotive will come off the train at Tebay to be replaced by a North Eastern Region locomotive that will take the train forward via Kirkby Stephen and Barnard Castle. This very successful class was originally designed by Henry Fowler for the Midland Railway and introduced in 1911. The LMS versions were introduced from 1924, and had detail differences. In all, the class numbered over 700 examples with No 44292 being built at Derby works in 1927 and withdrawn in 1963. *(ED Bruton)*

Wednesday 4th June 1952. Taken at the same site as the previous photograph, ex-LMS class 4 2-6-4 tank No 42432 leaves Oxenholme with the 5.00pm passenger train to Carlisle. Composed of ex-LNER coaching stock, the train was scheduled to take 1hr 24min to cover the 50 miles to Carlisle, inclusive of four intermediate stops. The locomotive was a Stanier version of the class constructed at Derby works in 1936, and it would be withdrawn in 1965. *(ED Bruton)*

Tuesday 11th November 1952. The forward-thinking Midland Railway had opened the Lancaster to Morecambe and Heysham routes to electric passenger trains in 1908 using a 6600V 25-cycle AC system. By 1951, the system was judged to be worn out and the electric stock was scrapped and replaced by steam trains. However, with the proposed electrification of the WCML, this compact system was converted to 25kv 50-cycle AC power, and was used as a test bed for some of the proposed equipment. The passenger stock used was some redundant ex-LNWR 3rd/4th rail units that had new English Electric equipment fitted. Here we see one of the converted 3-car units during the testing of the new system crossing the River Lune bridge on the approach to Lancaster Green Ayre station. This electric system became operational again during 1953, and was finally abandoned in January 1966 with DMUs taking over the passenger services. *(OOB Herbert)*

Wednesday 8th April 1953. Departing Penrith with a load of coke for Workington is class 2 2-6-0 No 46481. Built at Darlington in 1951, she is already looking uncared for, but will continue working until withdrawn in 1962 having given only 11 years' service. *(Eric Treacy, NRM)*

Friday 11th June 1954. Giants meet; it is approximately 3.30pm and the down Royal Scot has drawn into Carlisle station behind ex-LMS class 8P Princess Coronation 4-6-2 No 46247 *City of Liverpool*. She will uncouple from the train while classmate No 46221 *Queen Elizabeth* waits to couple up and take the train forward to Glasgow. *City of Liverpool* was built at Crewe works in 1943 as a streamlined version of the class, the casing being removed prior to Nationalisation. She would be withdrawn after only 20 years' service in 1963. *Queen Elizabeth* was one of the first of the class to be constructed in 1937 at Crewe works, again with streamlining that was later removed. She would also be withdrawn from service in 1963 after 26 years of service. *(N Caplan)*

Wednesday 4th August 1954. With the tower of Lancaster Priory and parish church in the background, this splendid photograph shows ex-LMS class 6P5F Patriot 4-6-0 No 45504 *Royal Signals* departing Lancaster station with the 1.30pm Barrow to Crewe train. Constructed at Crewe works in 1932, she would be withdrawn from service in 1962. *(JE Wilkinson)*

16

Thursday 26th August 1954. This southbound goods train passing through Lancaster Castle station is being hauled by ex-LMS class 5 4-6-0 No 44939 working hard with its heavy load. From one of the later batches of Black 5s to be built in 1945 at Horwich works, she would be withdrawn in 1965. Note the overhead catenary for the Morecambe and Heysham electrified system on the right. *(R Leslie)*

Saturday 4th September 1954. This photograph shows clearly the differences between two of the significant tank locomotive designs produced for the LMS. Henry Fowler's class 4 2-6-4 tank No 42401, built at Derby works in 1933, leads William Stanier's similar No 42427, also built at Derby works, but in 1936. They are seen hauling the 3.12pm Workington to Liverpool Exchange local leaving Ravenglass station. No 42401 was withdrawn in 1963, while No 42427 would be withdrawn in 1961. *(ED Bruton)*

Tuesday 7th September 1954. Constructed at Crewe works in 1950, Ivatt designed Mogul No 46457 is seen here departing Workington with the short, 2-coach, 2.20pm Workington to Keswick passenger train. The locomotive would be withdrawn during 1967. *(Ian S Pearsall)*

Wednesday 8th September 1954. The Whitehaven-Carlisle services were intensive with the 17 trains in each direction during weekdays being allowed 1hr 14min for the 40-mile journey with nine intermediate stops. On this day, Carlisle Upperby resident, ex-LMS class 2P 4-4-0 No 40412, is in charge of the 4.15pm Whitehaven to Carlisle service as it departs Aspatria station. The locomotive, based on a Johnson design, was built by Sharp Stewart & Co in 1892. She would be rebuilt on several occasions during her life, and would be withdrawn in 1959 after giving 67 years of service. *(Ian S Pearsall)*

Saturday 18th September 1954. An unidentified ex-LMS class 4 2-6-4 tank is approaching Hest Bank station leaving the water troughs in the background with a special Barrow to Morecambe working. Designed by Henry Fowler, this class of parallel-boilered tanks was introduced in 1927, and continued to be built until 1934, when the class reached 125 examples. *(H Armitage)*

Saturday 18th September 1954. All eyes are glued to the sight of the unique 3-cylinder Standard Pacific No 71000 *Duke of Gloucester* as she speeds through Hest Bank station at the head of the up Mid-Day Scot. Constructed only a few months earlier in 1954 as a replacement for locomotive No 46202 *Princess Anne*, which had been destroyed in the Harrow crash in 1952, she was allocated to Crewe North depot to work on the WCML. After withdrawal in 1962, she had a close encounter with a scrapyard, but survived to be purchased by a preservation group and returned to main line condition. *(H Armitage)*

Saturday 18th September 1954. The fireman on ex-LMS class 5 4-6-0 No 45348 has taken slightly too much water than necessary, so a sheet of spray is about to engulf the platforms at Hest Bank station as the locomotive speeds through with a Carlisle to Liverpool train. Built by Armstrong Whitworth in 1937, she would be withdrawn in 1966. *(H Armitage)*

Tuesday 9th November 1954. In preparation for the introduction of DMU services to the Carlisle to Silloth branch during the same month, several 2-car Derby Lightweight units were delivered to Carlisle Upperby depot for driver training. Here we see two 2-car units arriving ex-works at Upperby prior to these duties. *(JE Wilkinson)*

Saturday 12th February 1955. Ex-LMS class 8P Princess Coronation 4-6-2 No 46254 *City of Stoke-on-Trent* is getting into her stride at Brisco, about three miles south of Carlisle, with the 9.00am Perth to London express. Constructed at Crewe works in 1946, but as a non-streamlined example, she would be withdrawn after less than 20 years' service in 1964. *(R Leslie)*

Saturday 12th February 1955. With the remains of a recent snowfall still evident, ex-LMS class 4 2-6-4 tank No 42544 accelerates past Brisco, near Carlisle, with the 1.51pm Carlisle to Oxenholme "stopper". One of the Stanier-designed versions of this class she was constructed at Derby works in 1935 and would be withdrawn in 1962. *(R Leslie)*

Sunday 13th February 1955. Ex-LMS class 6P5F Jubilee 4-6-0 No 45671 *Prince Rupert* is seen here working a Glasgow to Manchester express past Brisco. Allocated to Newton Heath depot (26A), she was an example of this successful 3-cylinder class designed by William Stanier and introduced in 1934. Built at Crewe works in 1935, she would be withdrawn in 1963. *(R Leslie)*

Sunday 26th June 1955. What appears to be an excursion train made up of three 2-car Derby Lightweight DMUs traverses the spur from the Midland line to the North Eastern line at Appleby Junction, prior to working toward Penrith on the Eden Valley line. These units proved to be very successful and popular with the travelling public. *(Author's Collection)*

Tuesday 10th July 1956. Hest Bank station lay on the WCML between Lancaster and Carnforth and, although only provided with short platforms, it was served by Lancaster to Barrow local services. Sited just north of the station was a set of water troughs which provided a service for express trains. On this bright summer day, we see ex-LMS class 5 4-6-0 No 45054 working a Barrow to Manchester service. Built at the Vulcan Foundry, she was one of the earliest members of the class to be constructed in 1934, and she would not be withdrawn until 1968, making her one of the longest working members of her class. Towards the end of 1958, Hest Bank signalbox, seen behind the train, would be demolished during a resignalling programme, and would be replaced with a new box to the north of the station. *(Frank Wilde)*

Saturday 16th February 1957. Working hard with a goods train, ex-LMS class 8F 2-8-0 No 48761 pounds southbound through Calthwaite, south of Carlisle. Built at Doncaster works in 1946 as part of an order for the LNER, she was loaned to the LMS and finally taken into British Railways stock at Nationalisation. *(R Leslie)*

Thursday 5th September 1957. Working hard northbound with a Manchester/Liverpool to Glasgow/Edinburgh express is ex-LMS class 6P5F Jubilee 4-6-0 No 45635 *Tobago* as it nears the end of the climb to Shap summit. Built at Crewe works in 1934, she would give 30 years of service before being withdrawn during 1964. *(PH Groom)*

October 1957. Seen here passing Scout Green box with a down train of 6-wheeled milk tankers is ex-LMS class 2P 4-4-0 No 40653. One of the Crewe-built examples of the class, she was constructed in 1931 and fitted with a Dabeg feed water heater in 1933; she would be withdrawn in 1959. The Dabeg Automatic Locomotive Feed Pump was a patented apparatus to improve the efficiency of locomotives so fitted. By preheating the water feed with the use of exhaust steam, and using a mechanically-fitted pump system it was claimed that more water evaporation was gained when compared to conventional water injection methods, and therefore water and coal consumption were reduced. *(WJV Anderson)*

Saturday 21st June 1958. Ex-LMS class 2P 4-4-0 No 40683 is seen here piloting class 5 4-6-0 No 44735 at the head of a Manchester/Liverpool to Glasgow train approaching Hest Bank station. No 40683 was a Derby-built example of this class constructed in 1932, while the Black 5 was a post-Nationalisation example constructed at Crewe works in 1949; it would be withdrawn in 1968 and the 2P would be withdrawn during 1961. *(Frank Wilde)*

Sunday 6th July 1958. On this Sunday, engineering work at Hest Bank necessitated wrong line working. The 9.25am Glasgow to London Euston service headed by ex-LMS class 2P 4-4-0 No 40629 piloting Standard class 7P6F Britannia 4-6-2 No 70051 *Firth of Forth* has moved over to the down line while the engineers' train occupies the up line. The 2P was a Derby works example, built in 1931 and withdrawn in 1961, while *Firth of Forth* was one of the last Britannias to be constructed at Crewe works in 1954. She would be withdrawn after only 13 years of service during 1967. *(JB Welldon)*

Sunday 6th July 1958. Seen here climbing Shap with the down Royal Scot are the LMS-designed twin diesel electric locomotives Nos 10000 and 10001. Originally painted gloss black when they appeared from Derby works in 1947 and 1948, they were both repainted in Brunswick Green during 1956. *(R Leslie)*

Saturday 19th July 1958. An unusual pairing for a short Barrow to Preston passenger train is seen here at Hest Bank station. Class 5 4-6-0 No 44745, a Caprotti valve-gear fitted version of this successful class, is piloting Fowler-designed class 4 2-6-4 tank No 42317. The Black 5 was a post-Nationalisation example, constructed at Crewe in 1948, which would be withdrawn in 1964. The Fowler tank was a Derby works product of 1928, which would outlive the Black 5 to be withdrawn in 1965. Hest Bank station would close in February 1969. *(Frank Wilde)*

Wednesday 30th July 1958. This general view of Oxenholme depot shows a neat 4-road construction with a turntable at the rear of the shed. Simmering in front of the building is a Stanier-designed example of the ex-LMS class 4 2-6-4 tank No 42613 standing beside Black 5 No 45246. The tank was constructed by the NBL in 1937, while the Black 5 was a product of Armstrong Whitworth in 1936. Oxenholme depot would be closed in June 1962, and both locomotives would be withdrawn during 1967. *(A Brown)*

Thursday 31st July 1958. By this date, the Derby Lightweight DMUs delivered to Carlisle in 1954 were well-established operating services throughout west Cumberland. Here we see a 2-unit train, with car No M79009 leading, coming off the former Cockermouth, Keswick and Penrith Railway route at Penrith operating the 9.51am Workington to Carlisle service. Note that the driver is about to hand over the section token to the signalman. *(R Leslie)*

Saturday 28th March 1959. A splendid line up of pilot or banking locomotives is on display at Tebay depot with, from left to right, ex-LMS class 4 2-6-4 tanks Nos 42403, 42396 and 42424. All were built at Derby works, the former two in 1933 and the latter in 1934. The first two would be withdrawn in 1962, while 42424 would survive until 1964. Tebay depot was closed during 1968. *(A Brown)*

Saturday 23rd May 1959. Speeding through Lancaster Castle station at the head of the up Royal Scot are the LMS-designed diesel locomotives Nos 10000 and 10001. This same month, May 1959, would see the introduction of the English Electric designed and built Type 4 diesel locomotives to the London Midland Region. Conceived as part of the Modernisation Plan Pilot Scheme these were seen as the successors to Nos 10000 and 10001, and they went on to become reliable workhorses on both the East and West coast main lines. Meanwhile, the LMS-designed twins would start to spend more time out of use, and were eventually sold for scrap, 10000 being withdrawn in 1963 and 10001 being withdrawn in 1966. *(RJ Farrell)*

Saturday 18th July 1959. Looking well cared for by the staff at Bank Hall depot (27A), ex-LMS class 6P5F Patriot 4-6-0 No 45517 has just passed Hest Bank station with an afternoon Windermere to Liverpool Exchange working. An un-named member of this 3-cylinder class of locomotive, she was constructed at Crewe works in 1933 and would survive a further three years to be withdrawn during 1962. The track on the left of the photograph is the Hest Bank to Morecambe line which runs parallel to the WCML for a short distance before swinging away west to Bare Lane Junction. *(NA Machell)*

Saturday 1st August 1959. A somewhat menial task for a Pacific locomotive, Standard class 6P5F Clan 4-6-2 No 72005 Clan Macgregor eases through Settle Junction with a northbound train of empty open wagons. Built at Crewe works in 1952, she had a very short working life being withdrawn in 1962. *(Author's Collection)*

Saturday 1st August 1959. An example of Sir William Stanier's masterpiece Princess Coronation class is seen here working hard ascending Shap at Scout Green. With the 9.50am London Euston to Glasgow Central consisting of 15 coaches, no banking assistance has been taken, but the driver is making use of the steam sanders. No 46234 *Duchess of Abercorn* was constructed as a non-streamlined example of the class at Crewe works in 1938, and would be withdrawn during 1963 having given 25 years' service. *(JE Wilkinson)*

Wednesday 19th August 1959. Ex-LMS class 4 2-6-4 tank No 42589 is seen here departing Lakeside (Windermere) station with the branch train to Ulverston. A Stanier version of this class, she was built at the NBL in 1936 and would be withdrawn in 1964. The branch was opened in June 1869 and closed in September 1965 with the section between Lakeside and Haverthwaite reopened in May 1973 by the Lakeside and Haverthwaite Railway. This company now operates passenger trains on the 3½-mile section between those two stations and making connections with the steamers operating on Lake Windermere. *(RE Toop)*

Saturday 3rd October 1959. The principal LNWR heavy goods locomotive was of the 0-8-0 type of which almost 600 examples were built from 1892 onward, many being rebuilt several times during their life. Here we see No 48942 with a goods train between Morecambe South Junction and Lancaster. Allocated to Warrington depot (8F), she was constructed at Crewe works in 1903 as a class B 4-cylinder compound, later being converted to a 2-cylinder simple locomotive. She would give 58 years of service before being withdrawn in 1961. *(NA Machell)*

Tuesday 11th October 1959. Drifting down from Shap Summit with a goods train is ex-LMS class 5 4-6-0 No 45351, a Carlisle Kingmoor resident. Constructed by Armstrong Whitworth in 1937 she would be withdrawn during 1965. *(WS Sellar)*

Saturday 15th October 1959. An excellent study of ex-LMS class 7P Royal Scot 3-cylinder 4-6-0 No 46141 *The North Staffordshire Regiment* at Carlisle station as she departs with a Glasgow to Liverpool train. Originally designed by Sir Henry Fowler, and constructed by the NBL in 1927 with a parallel boiler, Sir William Stanier introduced a rebuilt version from 1943 onward, and from 1947 smoke deflectors were fitted to the class. This locomotive would be withdrawn during 1964.
(Spencer Yeates)

January 1960. Ex-works BR/Sulzer Type 2 No D5057 is seen here leaving Lancaster and heading south to Crewe on a trial run. Constructed at Crewe works in December 1959, this example of this highly successful design of locomotive would be withdrawn during 1978 numbered 24057. *(Nicholas F Scholes)*

Wednesday 1st June 1960. Seen here having just departed Staveley station with a Windermere to Oxenholme train is ex-LMS class 6P5F Patriot 4-6-0 No 45542. Constructed at Crewe in 1934, this un-named member of the class would be withdrawn in 1962. *(TG Hepburn)*

Tuesday 14th June 1960. Limping into Carlisle station 55 minutes late due to an engine failure is the 7.35am Aberdeen to Manchester Victoria train behind ex-LMS class 5 "Crab" 2-6-0 No 42836 piloting ex-LMS class 5, 4-6-0 No 44881. The Crab was a product of Horwich works in 1930, which would survive a further couple of years to be withdrawn during 1962, while the Black 5 was built at Crewe works in 1945, and would be withdrawn in 1966. *(A McBlain)*

Saturday 9th July 1960. This bright summer day sees ex-LMS class 6P5F Jubilee 4-6-0 No 45691 *Orion* working hard on Shap with a London to Glasgow relief. Built at Crewe in 1936, this example of this highly successful class would be withdrawn in 1962. *(T Boustead)*

Monday 8th August 1960. Another of the early successes of the Pilot Scheme were the BR/Sulzer Type 4 Peak locomotives which were introduced during 1959. No D5 *Cross Fell* is seen here passing the remains of Grayrigg station while working a down test train. Constructed at Derby works in October 1959, this locomotive would be withdrawn in 1978 numbered 44005. Grayrigg station had been closed to passenger traffic in February 1954. *(Derek Cross)*

Tuesday 16th August 1960. Ivatt-designed class 2 2-6-0 No 46455 waits to enter the single line section from Keswick to Penrith as a Penrith to Workington diesel service operated by a Derby Lightweight set approaches the station. The Mogul was built at Crewe works in 1950, and would be withdrawn in 1967. *(RJ Farrell)*

Sunday 25th September 1960. Working hard on the ascent of Shap, ex-LMS class 8P Princess Royal 4-6-2 No 46200 *Princess Royal* is hauling a 12-coach London Euston to Glasgow Central train without the assistance of a banker. One of Sir William Stanier's earliest successes, this would be the first example of a class of thirteen locomotives constructed at Crewe works in 1933. She would be the last of the class to be withdrawn in 1962.
(Derek Singleton)

35

Sunday 6th November 1960. Heading a Glasgow to Birmingham express is ex-LMS class 8P Princess Coronation 4-6-2 No 46241 *City of Edinburgh*. Seen at speed in the open countryside between Southwaite and Calthwaite, this example of the class was originally constructed at Crewe in 1940 with a streamlined casing which would be removed prior to Nationalisation. She would be withdrawn in 1964. *(R Leslie)*

Saturday 13th May 1961. With the imposing bulk of Wild Boar Fell in the background, ex-WD class 8F 2-8-0 No 90012 is about to pass Ais Gill summit at the head of a southbound goods train from Carlisle. The locomotive bears a 55E (Normanton) shed code. Built as part of a Ministry of Supply order for wartime service, this example was constructed by the NBL in 1943, numbered 7211 (later 77211) by the War Department, and shipped to France in 1945. She would be returned to the UK during 1946 and allocated to the LNER, being purchased from the Ministry of Supply by British Railways during 1948 along with over 700 other examples of the class. *(R Leslie)*

Sunday 28th May 1961. Beginning the descent of Hest Bank is ex-LMS class 8P Princess Coronation 4-6-2 No 46249 *City of Sheffield* at the head of a Glasgow to Birmingham express. Built at Crewe works in 1944 as a non-streamlined example of the class, she would be withdrawn after only 19 years' service in 1963. *(NA Machell)*

Saturday 3rd June 1961. Ex-LMS class 7P Royal Scot 4-6-0 No 46129 *The Scottish Horse* is in charge of a London Euston to Barrow and Workington train as it passes Morecambe South Junction. Originally designed by Henry Fowler and constructed by the NBL in 1927 with a parallel boiler, this locomotive would be rebuilt in 1944 with a taper boiler and would be withdrawn in 1964. *(NA Machell)*

Wednesday 28th June 1961. Deep within the Lune Gorge, the fireman operating the water scoop on ex-LMS class 6P5F Patriot 4-6-0 No 45551 is about to run out of water at the Dillicar troughs near Tebay. Meanwhile, the vans comprising this southbound goods train are receiving an unexpected soaking. *(Derek Cross)*

July 1961. This spectacular photograph gives a flavour of the hard work performed by the Henry Fowler designed 3-cylinder Patriot class. Seen in the open countryside near Shap Wells with a London Euston to Glasgow express consisting of twelve coaches, No 45551, an unnamed member of the class, is tackling the climb to Shap summit without the assistance of a banker. The last of the class to be constructed at Crewe works in 1934, she would be withdrawn from service in 1962. *(Peter J Robinson)*

Saturday 29th July 1961. At Whitehaven Bransty station, class 6P5F Jubilee 4-6-0 No 45652 *Hawke* waits to depart with a Workington to Carnforth local. Built at Crewe works in 1935, this locomotive had a working life of 30 years before being withdrawn in 1965. *(WS Sellar)*

Sunday 30th July 1961. Ex-LMS class 7P Royal Scot 4-6-0 No 46104 *Scottish Borderer* is rounding the curve between Eden Valley Junction and Clifton and Lowther station with a Glasgow to Liverpool express. Constructed as one of the original batch of locomotives at the NBL in 1927, she would be rebuilt with a taper boiler in 1946 and withdrawn during 1962. *(R Leslie)*

Monday 14th August 1961. The Lakeside branch daily goods train is seen departing from Haverthwaite on its return to Ulverston behind veteran ex-MR Johnson-designed 2F 0-6-0 No 58177. Built by Neilson & Co as far back as 1876, it soldiered on for a further year to be withdrawn during 1962, having given 86 years of service. *(JC Hayden)*

Tuesday 15th August 1961. Class 5 4-6-0 No 44713 is seen pulling away from the down loop at Tebay with the 5.28am Crewe to Carlisle goods. The permanent way gangers working on some pointwork are engrossed in their duties and ignore its passing. Built at Horwich works in 1948, it would only survive 20 years before being withdrawn in 1968. *(JC Hayden)*

Saturday 19th August 1961. With admiring enthusiasts noting details, ex-LMS class 6P5F Jubilee 4-6-0 No 45596 *Bahamas*, looking very clean, pauses in Carlisle station with a southbound express. Constructed by the NBL in 1935, this locomotive had been fitted with a double chimney earlier in 1961 and would be withdrawn in 1966. She was purchased by the Bahamas Locomotive Society in 1967, and is currently based at the Keighley and Worth Valley Railway. *(WS Sellar)*

Monday 11th September 1961. BR/Sulzer Type 4 No D42 departs Lancaster Green Ayre station with the 6.48pm Morecambe Promenade to Leeds City passenger train. Having left Derby works only a month earlier, and been allocated to Derby depot, it would be withdrawn in 1987 numbered 45034, to be moved into departmental stock as number 97411. It would finally be scrapped during 1992. *(NA Machell)*

Monday 25th September 1961. The down Royal Scot is seen here passing the remains of Grayrigg station hauled by English Electric Type 4 No D296. Built at the Vulcan Foundry in 1960, it would be withdrawn in 1983 numbered 40096. *(Derek Cross)*

Friday 2nd March 1962. Class 2 2-6-0 No 46422 has arrived at Glasson Dock on the River Lune estuary to make up a train of empty wagons destined for Lancaster. Built at Crewe works in 1948, this locomotive would only give 18 years' service before being withdrawn in 1966. Glasson Dock had been the site of several shipbuilding and repair yards throughout its history, but by the 1960s it was a graving dock which also scrapped some steam locomotives. Passenger traffic had ceased in July 1930, and the branch finally closed to all traffic in September 1964. Note the 3-masted sailing ship in the background. Named Moby Dick, it was later destroyed by fire. *(Ron Herbert)*

Saturday 14th April 1962. English Electric Type 4 No D319 is seen departing Lancaster with an afternoon Glasgow to Manchester service. This was one of the few examples of the class built at the Robert Stephenson and Hawthorn works in 1961, and it would be withdrawn in 1980 numbered 40119. *(NA Machell)*

Friday 27th April 1962. Ivatt-designed class 4 2-6-0 No 43028 bears no legible identification marks bar the smokebox number plate. She was constructed at Horwich works in 1949 with a double chimney which was later replaced by a single version. Seen here at Ravenglass, she is waiting to return to Workington with a special excursion. The locomotive would only give 18 years' service before being withdrawn in 1967. *(Ron Herbert)*

Thursday 2nd August 1962. Class 4 2-6-4 tank No 42136 is slowing down to stop at Greenodd station with a passenger train from Lakeside to Ulverston. This locomotive was a Fairburn example of this numerous class and was built at Derby works in 1950, only to be withdrawn in 1963 after 13 years of service. Note the unusual style of brick banding used in the station buildings. *(R Jeannes)*

Saturday 18th August 1962. The driver of this 2-car Derby Lightweight DMU is preparing to pick up the token from the signalman at Penrith No 1 box to enable him to proceed onto the Keswick branch with this service for Workington. *(Derek Cross)*

Friday 31st August 1962. With a train of tank wagons from Stourton in tow, ex-LMS class 5 "Crab" 2-6-0 No 42776 is approaching Heysham Moss. One of the 1927-constructed Crewe works examples of the class, she would be withdrawn in 1964. *(Ron Herbert)*

Monday 24th December 1962. This splendidly atmospheric photograph shows an Edinburgh to Birmingham express speeding toward Southwaite behind a very clean ex-LMS class 5 4-6-0 No 45247 that bears a 6H (Bangor) shed code. Built by Armstrong Whitworth in 1936, it would survive a further five years to be withdrawn during 1967. *(Peter J Robinson)*

Saturday 23rd March 1963. One of the failures of the Pilot Scheme, Metropolitan-Vickers Type 2 No D5707 accelerates the 10.53am Workington to London Euston train past Morecambe South Junction. Built at their Stockton-on-Tees works, they were powered by a Crossley two-stroke diesel engine which proved unreliable. They were initially allocated to operate the Condor overnight container service between Hendon and Glasgow, but the 20 members of the class were finally allocated to the Barrow area where they finished their working lives. This example was constructed in 1958, and would be withdrawn only ten years later in 1968. *(NA Machell)*

Saturday 13th April 1963. Having been stopped earlier in her progress up the bank, this splendid study shows ex-LMS class 5 4-6-0 No 45024 climbing the northern slopes of Shap with a down goods train. One of the earlier examples of this successful class constructed at the Vulcan Foundry in 1934, she survived 33 years to be withdrawn in 1967. *(D Ian Wood)*

Friday 13th September 1963. Leaving Carlisle station with a full head of steam is ex-LMS class 8P Princess Coronation 4-6-2 No 46225 *Duchess of Gloucester* at the head of the 12.25pm Perth to London Euston train. Built at Crewe works in 1938 as a streamlined example of the class, she would have the casing removed at the end of the Second World War and would be withdrawn during 1964. *(WS Sellar)*

Tuesday 7th April 1964. Having just come off the turntable at Keswick, class 2 2-6-0 No 46488 poses for the camera before moving away for her next duty. Constructed at Darlington works in 1951 she would be withdrawn during 1965. *(GNG Tingey)*

Saturday 27th July 1963. In the crisp still morning air, the exhausted steam from two locomotives leaves a fascinating trail as they ascend Shap near Scout Green. Ex-LMS class 4 2-6-4 tank No 42571 is piloting ex-LMS class 7P Royal Scot 4-6-0 No 46162 *Queen's Westminster Riflemen* with a Llandovery to Glasgow troop train. No 42571 was a Stanier variation of the class built by the NBL in 1936, which would be withdrawn four months later. The Royal Scot was one of the Derby-built examples constructed in 1930, which would be rebuilt in 1948 and withdrawn during 1964. *(Derek Cross)*

Friday 13th September 1963. Seen here waiting to depart Carlisle with the 1.30pm Fridays-only Manchester to Glasgow working is ex-LMS class 7P Royal Scot 4-6-0 No 46160 *Queen Victoria's Rifleman*. Constructed in 1930 at Derby works, and rebuilt in 1945, she would be withdrawn in 1965. Note the solitary lamp on the bufferbeam – the fireman has yet to change the lamp code, or has he forgotten? *(WS Sellar)*

Friday 26th July 1963. An increasingly common scene at this time when diesel locomotives were replacing steam power on passenger duties, and steam was being relegated to secondary work. At the southern end of Penrith yard, ex-LMS class 8P Princess Coronation 4-6-2 No 46229 *Duchess of Hamilton* waits in the down loop with a northbound parcels train, while English Electric Type 4 No D215 *Aquitania* speeds north with a Liverpool to Glasgow passenger train. Built at the Vulcan Foundry in 1959, the Type 4 would be withdrawn in 1984 numbered 40015. However, *Duchess of Hamilton* would survive to become a major attraction in the preservation scene. Constructed at Crewe works in 1938 as a streamlined version of the class, she was shipped to the New York World's Fair in 1939 disguised as No 6220 *Coronation*. After this, she toured the United States before her return to the UK in 1943 when she re-acquired her original identity. The streamlined casing would later be removed, and she would be withdrawn from service in 1964 to be bought by Butlins for display at their Minehead Camp. In 1980, she was overhauled and returned to the main line again for many years before her boiler certificate expired. She is currently to be seen at the NRM in York wearing the replacement streamline casing fitted during 2009. The Type 4 was named after the Cunard liner of the same name launched in 1913, which served as a hospital ship during the First World War. The liner would be scrapped in 1950. *(Derek Cross)*

Friday 26th July 1963. Threading its way through the Westmorland Fells at the head of a northbound parcels train near Oxenholme is English Electric Type 4 No D216 *Campania*. Constructed at the Vulcan Foundry in 1959, it would be withdrawn in 1981 numbered 40016. The locomotive was named after a Cunard liner that was launched in 1892, only to be sunk after a collision in November 1918. *(Derek Cross)*

Saturday 6th July 1963. Ex-LMS class 4 2-6-4 tank No 42449 is seen near Kendal while working the 4.55pm Windermere to Oxenholme train. One of the Stanier-designed examples of this class, she was constructed at Derby works in 1936, and would be withdrawn from service in 1964. *(Gerald T Robinson)*

Saturday 13th July 1963. With a spectacular backdrop of the Westmorland Fells, Standard class 6P5F Clan 4-6-2 No 72009 *Clan Stewart* heads a down Blackpool to Balloch special through the Lune valley. The last of ten examples of the class to be constructed at Crewe works in 1952, she would be withdrawn after only 13 years of service in 1965. *(Derek Cross)*

July 1963. This bright summer day sees ex-LMS class 7P Rebuilt Patriot 4-6-0 No 45545 *Planet* working a down passenger train for Glasgow past Oxenholme. Originally built at Crewe works in 1934 as a Henry Fowler designed Patriot class locomotive, it would be rebuilt with a taper boiler, new cylinders and a double chimney under the direction of HG Ivatt during 1948. She would be one of the last examples of the class to be withdrawn in 1964. (*Eric Oldham*)

Thursday 4th July 1963. The 7.40pm train for Lancaster Castle station waits to depart Morecambe Promenade with EMU car No M28220M leading. When British Railways re-introduced the electric passenger services between Lancaster and Morecambe and Heysham in 1953, they used converted ex-LNWR 1914-built 3rd/4th rail stock which had been in store throughout the Second World War. (*Leslie Sandler*)

Tuesday 28th May 1963. Approaching Shap summit with a down crew-training special is BR/Sulzer Type 4 No D57 in ex-works condition. Built at Crewe works and only days into its service life, it would be withdrawn in 1985 numbered 45042. *(Derek Cross)*

Saturday 8th June 1963. Waiting at Carlisle station to take over a down Scottish express is Standard class 6P5F Clan 4-6-2 No 72008 *Clan Macleod*. Built at Crewe in 1952, she would be withdrawn after only 14 years' service in 1966. Although none of the class survived into preservation, the Standard Steam Locomotive Co is currently building what will be the 11th member of the class, 72010 *Hengist*. *(IS Carr)*

Tuesday 7th May 1963. Class 2 2-6-0 No 46432 is plodding past Derwent Junction signalbox at Workington with a down mineral train consisting of hopper wagons. The locomotive was of post-Nationalisation construction at Crewe works in 1948 which would be withdrawn in 1967. The line diverging to the right of the photograph leads to Workington docks while the line in the middle background diverging to the left is the ex-LNWR line to Cockermouth. *(NA Machell)*

Wednesday 8th May 1963. The quiet rural atmosphere is apparent here as the 9.45am Workington to Carlisle service via Penrith is seen leaving Threlkeld station on the former Cockermouth, Keswick and Penrith Railway route. The 2-car Derby Lightweight DMU has by this time acquired a yellow warning panel. *(NA Machell)*

Friday 3rd May 1963. Metropolitan-Vickers Type 2 No D5702 is seen departing Carnforth at the head of the 5.45pm Liverpool Exchange to Millom and Whitehaven train. Built in 1958 this locomotive has 12E painted on the bufferbeam indicating that it is allocated to Barrow depot. It would be withdrawn from service during 1968. *(NA Machell)*

Saturday 4th May 1963. This unusually powerful combination of two ex-WD class 8F 2-8-0s is seen near Dillicar hauling a train of track panels from Fazakerley to Southwaite with No 90366 leading No 90328. Both Locomotives were constructed at the NBL in 1944 as part of a Ministry of Supply order, and they would both later be shipped to France for service with the Allied Forces there. The former was numbered 8521 (later 78521) and the latter numbered 845 (later 70845) by the War Department. On return to the UK, both locomotives would be purchased by British Railways during 1948, and both would be withdrawn from service in 1964. *(Ron Herbert)*

Thursday 9th April 1964. At the head of the down Royal Scot, English Electric Type 4 No D214 *Antonia* picks up water for its steam heating boiler as it passes over Dillicar troughs. This locomotive was built at the Vulcan Foundry in 1959, and would be withdrawn during 1981 numbered 40014. Another of the class named after Cunard liners, the ship was launched in 1921 and scrapped in 1948. *(Eric Treacy, NRM)*

Saturday 15th May 1964. Brush Type 4 No D1570, bearing a 55A (Leeds Holbeck) shed code, pauses at Lancaster Green Ayre station with the 9.33am Morecambe to Leeds passenger train. Only two months old, and still looking in ex-works condition, it would give 25 years of service before being withdrawn in 1989 numbered 47017. *(MS Welch)*

Saturday 15th May 1964. Accelerating through Lancaster Castle station is ex-LMS class 5 "Crab" 2-6-0 No 42901 with an up fitted goods train. One of the 1930 Crewe-built examples of this successful class, she would be withdrawn during 1965. *(MS Welch)*

Sunday 23rd May 1964. Approaching Heysham with a service from Lancaster is 3-car EMU with No M29022M leading. Converted from ex-LNWR stock, and introduced to the line during 1953, these units would continue to work the route until the electric service was withdrawn in 1966. *(Ian G Holt)*

Thursday 27th May 1964. This splendid photograph shows ex-LMS class 5 4-6-0 No 44834 taking water at Dillicar troughs while hurrying north with a Crewe to Carlisle goods train. Watching its passage is a permanent way gang undertaking some maintenance work on the up section of the troughs. The Black 5 was constructed at Crewe works in 1940, and would be withdrawn in 1967. *(JR Carter)*

Saturday 13th June 1964. Leaving Tebay station in the background, ex-WD class 8F 2-8-0 No 90142 crosses the River Lune with an up fitted goods train. Built by the NBL in 1943 and numbered 7150 (later 77150) by the War Department, she would serve with Allied Forces in Europe, and on return the UK be bought by British Railways in 1948. She would be withdrawn from service in 1965. *(John K Morton)*

Saturday 13th June 1964. The 4.41pm Carlisle to Silloth service pauses at Burgh-by-Sands. This part of the 22½-mile branch was opened by the Carlisle and Port Carlisle Railway in 1853, and was extended to Silloth in 1856. DMU operation was introduced in November 1954 using 2-car Derby Lightweight units, and the line was closed to passenger traffic in September 1964 as part of the Beeching closures. *(WS Sellar)*

Saturday 13th June 1964. Looking in splendid condition, ex-LMS class 8P Princess Coronation 4-6-2 No 46238 *City of Carlisle* is the standby locomotive at Upperby depot on this day. Constructed at Crewe works in 1939 as a streamlined example of the class, the casing would be removed during 1947. She would be withdrawn only a few months after this photograph was taken. *(WS Sellar)*

Saturday 20th June 1964. At Kendal station, a Fairburn example of the class 4 2-6-4 tank No 42198 pauses with a Windermere to Oxenholme train. Built at Derby works in 1948, she would be withdrawn during 1965. Opened through from Oxenholme to Windermere in April 1847, the branch would be reduced to a single track during 1972/3.
(Author)

Saturday 27th June 1964. Ex-LMS class 5 4-6-0 No 45131 is struggling with a northbound parcels train on the climb away from Tebay. The photographer noted that the locomotive took approximately 25 minutes to complete the ascent to Shap summit. Constructed by Armstrong Whitworth in 1935, she would be withdrawn in 1968.
(JS Whiteley)

Saturday 4th July 1964. A commonplace sight at this time was a diesel locomotive piloting a steam locomotive on some of the heavier loaded passenger trains. BR/Sulzer Type 2 No D5133 is assisting ex-LMS class 6P5F Jubilee 4-6-0 No 45627 *Sierra Leone* with the 9.00am Perth to London Euston train as it enters Carlisle station. D5133 was built at Derby works in 1960, and would be withdrawn numbered 24133 in 1978, while the Jubilee was constructed at Crewe works in 1934, and would be withdrawn during 1966. *(WS Sellar)*

Sunday 12th July 1964. Seen here at Tebay station working the Stephenson Locomotive Society's "Pacific Pennine Railtour" from Birmingham is ex-LMS class 8P Princess Coronation 4-6-2 No 46251 *City of Nottingham*. Built as an non-streamlined example of the class at Crewe works in 1944, she would be withdrawn three months after this photograph was taken. *(WS Sellar)*

Saturday 18th July 1964. Moving a train of limestone hoppers out of Shap Quarry siding is ex-LMS class 8F 2-8-0 No 48399. Constructed at Horwich works in 1945, she would be withdrawn in 1967. *(AW Martin)*

August 1964. The locomotive for the 7.12am Garsdale to Hellifield local is taking water before departing. Class 2 2-6-2 tank No 41251 is almost ready to leave Garsdale with this early morning train that connects at Hellifield with a Heysham to Leeds service. Constructed at Crewe works in 1949, she would be withdrawn after only 17 years of service in 1966. Garsdale had been the junction for the scenic cross-country Wensleydale line to Northallerton which had been closed in sections during 1954 and 1959. *(Andrew Muckley)*

Monday 10th August 1964. This 2.55pm service from Penrith to Workington is seen between Threlkeld and Keswick being operated by a 2-car Derby Lightweight DMU with car number M79607 leading. *(John Clarke)*

Monday 10th August 1964. Standard class 6P5F Clan 4-6-2 No 72007 *Clan Macintosh* is seen passing Kingmoor depot at Carlisle with the 9.25am Crewe to Perth and Aberdeen service. Built at Crewe works in 1952, she would be withdrawn during 1965. *(JS Whiteley)*

Monday 10th August 1964. A 3-car EMU, with car No M28221M leading, departs Lancaster Green Ayre station with the 6.40pm service from Morecambe Promenade to Lancaster Castle. Note the modern style pantograph fitted to this unit. *(RF Roberts, SLS)*

Monday 10th August 1964. A 3-car EMU, with car No M29022M leading, waits to depart Lancaster Castle station with the 7.25pm service to Morecambe Promenade and Heysham. *(RF Roberts, SLS)*

Thursday 20th August 1964. Through coaches from London Euston to Workington had been a feature of the former Cockermouth, Keswick and Penrith route since the late 19th century, with both the LNWR and the LMS promoting this popular summer service as "The Lakes Express". British Railways continued the through service until 1966, when it was withdrawn from the timetable. This scene at Cockermouth station shows class 2 2-6-0 No 46432, bearing a 12D (Kirkby Stephen) shed code, waiting to depart with the up "Lakes Express" to Penrith. Built in 1948 at Crewe works, this locomotive would be withdrawn during 1967. *(Derek Cross)*

Thursday 20th August 1964. The late evening sunshine highlights the smokebox of class 2 2-6-0 No 46432 as she pauses at Keswick station with the down "Lakes Express" to Workington. *(Derek Cross)*

Thursday 20th August 1964. Ex-LMS class 5 4-6-0 No 45226 is held at Derwent Junction, Workington, while working a southbound train of hopper wagons loaded with coke. Passing on the down line is a Whitehaven to Carlisle service being operated by a 2-car Derby Lightweight DMU. The Black 5 was constructed by Armstrong Whitworth in 1936, and would be withdrawn from service in 1967. *(Derek Cross)*

Monday 24th August 1964. Class 5 4-6-0 No 44730 accelerates away from Carnforth station with the 8.45pm Blackpool to Windermere working. Built at Crewe works in 1949, this locomotive would be withdrawn during 1967. *(JB Mounsey)*

Monday 24th August 1964. An unusual pairing with a local goods working leaves Carnforth southbound. Ex-LMS class 3F "Jinty" 0-6-0 tank No 47662 is piloting classmate No 47317. The former had been built by Beardmore Ltd in 1929, while the latter had been constructed by the NBL in 1926; both locomotives would be withdrawn during 1966. The original design for this class dated from the Johnson period at the Midland Railway, but Henry Fowler continued the design for the LMS as its standard shunting locomotive, and over 400 examples were built by a number of manufacturers. *(JB Mounsey)*

Friday 28th August 1964. Sir Williams Stanier's first main line design for the LMS after his arrival from the GWR was a class 5 Mogul introduced in 1933. Only 40 examples were constructed, as the design was superseded by his highly successful class 5 4-6-0 introduced in 1934, which became known as Black 5. The example of the Mogul seen here is No 42961 working an up goods train through the heavily wooded countryside near Thrimby Grange, north of Shap. Allocated to Springs Branch Wigan (8F), she was built at Crewe works in 1934, and would be withdrawn in 1965. *(MS Welch)*

Saturday 29th August 1964. Standard class 6P5F Clan 4-6-2 No 72006 *Clan Mackenzie* accelerates away from Lancaster with an up Carlisle to Patricroft goods train. Built at Crewe works in 1952, she was allocated to Carlisle Kingmoor depot, and became the last of the class to be withdrawn from service in 1966. *(NA Machell)*

Sunday 30th August 1964. Working hard past the remains of Grayrigg station is ex-LMS class 4 2-6-4 tank No 42680 piloting Standard class 7P6F Britannia 4-6-2 No 70006 *Robert Burns* with the 13-coach 9.30 am Manchester to Glasgow passenger train. The tank was one of the Fairburn variants of the class built at Derby in 1945, and she would be withdrawn after 20 years' service in 1965. The Britannia was one of the earlier members of the class coming out of Crewe works in 1951 and working until 1967, before being withdrawn. *(Harold D Bowtell)*

Sunday 30th August 1964. This delightful station and its setting are at Kirkandrews on the branch from Carlisle to Silloth. BRC&W Type 2 No D5305 is arriving with a train for Silloth. This class of locomotive was another success of the Pilot Scheme, when introduced initially on the Eastern Region in 1958. This example was built in 1958 and would be withdrawn in 1993 numbered 26005. *(Derek Cross)*

Monday 31st August 1964. This Manchester to Glasgow passenger train is seen departing Lancaster Castle station behind English Electric Type 4 No D255. Constructed at the Vulcan Foundry in 1960, it would later be numbered 40055 in British Railways' TOPS scheme, and was withdrawn in 1982. *(Frank Wilde)*

September 1964. Ex-LMS class 5 4-6-0 No 44937 is looking very clean at the head of the 4.24pm Sundays-only Carlisle to Manchester stopping train as it passes Carlisle No 12 box. Built at Horwich works in 1945, she would be withdrawn in 1967. *(Peter J Robinson)*

Sunday 6th September 1964. On the last day of passenger services on the Carlisle to Silloth branch, BRC&W Type 2 No D5310 pulls away from Port Carlisle Junction with a train for Silloth. This locomotive was built in 1959, and would be withdrawn in 1992 numbered 26010 and sold to a private buyer. It is currently based at the Llangollen Railway. *(Derek Cross)*

Saturday 12th September 1964. Ex-LMS class 8F 2-8-0 No 48115 tackles the 1 in 98 climb out of Lancaster Castle at the head of a Carlisle to Patricroft goods train. Constructed at Crewe in 1939, she would be one of the last of the class to be withdrawn in July 1968. *(NA Machell)*

Saturday 19th September 1964. Leaving in its wake an enormous cloud of smoke and steam as it labours on the approach to Halton on the Midland line from Lancaster to Settle Junction, ex-LMS class 5 4-6-0 No 44948 is working a Heysham Harbour to Stourton (near Leeds) fitted goods train. Built at Horwich works in 1946, she would be withdrawn during 1967. *(NA Machell)*

Wednesday 23rd September 1964. Ex-LMS class 5 4-6-0 No 45408 is seen passing Carnforth No 1 Junction box as it proceeds south with the 6.38am Workington to London passenger train. This Black 5 was constructed by Armstrong Whitworth in 1937, and would be withdrawn in 1966. The Carnforth depot coaling tower can be seen on the skyline in the background. *(NA Machell)*

Wednesday 23rd September 1964. Standard class 5 4-6-0 No 73136 is seen near Over Kellet on the former Furness and Midland Railways' joint line from Carnforth to Wennington while hauling the 10.35am Carnforth to Leeds train. This locomotive was one of a batch of 30 examples of the class constructed at Derby works during 1956/7, and fitted with Caprotti valve gear in an attempt to increase the efficiency of maintenance. She would be withdrawn after only 12 years' service in 1968. Note the Thompson-designed coach immediately behind the locomotive. *(NA Machell)*

Tuesday 29th September 1964. Ex-LMS class 4 0-6-0 No 44149, fitted with a self-weighing tender, tackles the climb out of Lancaster with a train of tank wagons from Heysham to Tees. It is approaching Halton on the former Midland Railway line from Lancaster to Settle Junction. Built at Crewe works in 1925, she would be withdrawn from service just two months after this photograph was taken. Note the list of tolls payable for the use of the crossing and the Midland Railway trespass notice. *(NA Machell)*

October 1964. The fireman working on Standard class 7P6F Britannia 4-6-2 No 70001 *Lord Hurlcomb* must have worked up a good fire as the locomotive is blowing-off as it passes Greenholme in the lower reaches of the ascent to Shap. This could, however, be attributed to the banker doing a good job. The Britannia was the second Standard locomotive to come out of Crewe works in 1951, and she gave 15 years of service before being withdrawn in 1966. *(WJV Anderson)*

Saturday 3rd October 1964. The fireman on this Black 5 is apparently taking a breather from his shovelling as the results of his work darken the skies above him. Ex-LMS class 5 4-6-0 No 45140, built by Armstrong Whitworth in 1935, is working southbound out of Carlisle with a goods train. The locomotive would be withdrawn in 1966. *(AR Thompson)*

Tuesday 13th October 1964. A 3-car EMU, with car No M28222M leading, is departing Scale Hall station while working on the Morecambe to Lancaster system. Note the different pantograph fitted to this unit compared to that on car No M28221M on page 63. *(Ian S Pearsall)*

Saturday 28th November 1964. Standard class 4 2-6-0 No 76084 is obliterating the surrounding landscape near Cumwhitton on the former Midland Railway line out of Carlisle while working an up goods train. Built at Horwich works in 1957, she was withdrawn only ten years later and moved to Woodham's scrapyard at Barry where she lay for many years until purchased for preservation in 1983. The locomotive is currently based at the North Norfolk Railway. *(WAC Smith)*

Saturday 20th March 1965. During a heavy shower of rain, Standard class 4 4-6-0 No 75039 pauses at Wennington station while working the 12.22pm Saturdays-only Skipton to Heysham passenger train. Wennington was also the junction for the former Furness and Midland Joint line to Carnforth. The locomotive was a product of Swindon works in 1953, and would be withdrawn in 1967. *(WS Sellar)*

Saturday 15th May 1965. This impressive photograph of Standard class 6P5F Clan 4-6-2 No 72006 *Clan Mackenzie* shows her coming off the Ribblehead Viaduct at the head of the 8.05am Carlisle to Hellifield "stopper". Seen here minus nameplates, she would be withdrawn from service the following year. *(Paul Riley)*

July 1965. Standard class 9F 2-10-0 No 92166 is near Tebay early on this morning heading a down goods train; the photographer noted that the sheeted open wagons contained reels of paper. This 9F was built at Crewe works in 1958, and only had a working life of nine years before being withdrawn in 1967. *(WJV Anderson)*

Friday 2nd July 1965. Ex-LMS class 5 4-6-0 No 45322 is pictured here at Carlisle station working an up train consisting of 6-wheeled milk tankers. This Black 5 was constructed by Armstrong Whitworth in 1937, and would be withdrawn during 1966. *(N Caplan)*

Friday 2nd July 1965. BR/Sulzer Type 4 No D93 is waiting to leave Carlisle Kingmoor depot. Built at Crewe works in 1961, it would be withdrawn in 1985 numbered 45057 in the BR TOPS scheme. *(N Caplan)*

Friday 2nd July 1965. An interesting comparison standing on the centre roads at Carlisle station. A 2-car Derby Lightweight DMU, introduced to the West Cumberland route services in 1954, represents the modern era, while in the adjoining road the older era is represented by class 2 2-6-2 tank No 41217, which was built at Crewe works only six years earlier than the DMU, and was fitted for working push-pull trains. The tank locomotive would be withdrawn in 1966 having served 18 years, but surprisingly the last of the Derby Lightweight units were withdrawn during 1969 having served only 15 years. *(N Caplan)*

Saturday 17th July 1965. On this bright summer day, ex-LMS class 5 4-6-0 No 45295 is seen taking water at Garsdale troughs while working a Glasgow to Leeds excursion. An Armstrong Whitworth constructed example of the class from December 1936, she would complete over 30 years of service before being withdrawn in December 1967. *(Maurice S Burns)*

Saturday 17th July 1965. This photograph, taken at Carlisle Kingmoor depot, offers a good comparison of two successful classes of express locomotive. On the left is one of Sir Nigel Gresley's 1936 3-cylinder class V2s, designed to operate express goods trains throughout the LNER system, but which went on to become a sure-footed workhorses on both fast goods and express passenger traffic. This example, No 60813, was constructed at Darlington works in 1937 and fitted with a short stovepipe chimney; she would be withdrawn in 1966. On the right is an example of the first Standard locomotive class introduced by British Railways in 1951. Class 7P6F Britannia 4-6-2 No 70009 *Alfred the Great* came out of Crewe works in May 1951, and spent much of her working life based at Norwich working express passenger trains to London. After being displaced by the introduction of English Electric Type 4 diesels on this route, she would be moved to the northern section of the LMR from where she was withdrawn in 1967. *(WS Sellar)*

Saturday 17th July 1965. Another success of the British Railways Standard classes was the class 5 4-6-0. Here we see No 73059 passing Kingmoor depot in Carlisle while working an up express. Allocated to Polmadie depot in Glasgow, she was built at Derby works in 1954, and would be withdrawn in 1967. *(WS Sellar)*

Saturday 17th July 1965. Seen here at Greenholme on the climb to Shap Summit, is ex-LMS class 5 4-6-0 No 45057 at the head of the Scottish-bound Ford car carrier. One of the earlier built examples from the Vulcan Foundry, she entered service during December 1934, and would serve almost 33 years before being withdrawn during August 1967. *(Maurice S Burns)*

Thursday 29th July 1965. Ex-LMS class 5 4-6-0 No 44915 is making light work of the ascent of Shap with the Keswick and Workington portion of the down "Lakes Express". Built at Crewe works in 1945, she would be withdrawn from service in 1967. *(MS Welch)*

August 1965. An unusual pairing is seen here at Penrith preparing to depart with a down goods. Class 2 2-6-0 No 46434 is piloting Standard class 9F 2-10-0 No 92161 for the run down to Carlisle. The Mogul was constructed at Crewe works in 1948, and would be withdrawn in 1966, while the 9F was also a product of Crewe in 1957. It would also be withdrawn in 1966, lasting only nine years. *(WJV Anderson)*

Friday 27th August 1965. With the impressive bulk of Lonscale Fell towering in the background, a 2-car Derby Lightweight DMU wends its way through the valley of the River Greta having just departed Keswick with the 15.20 service from Workington to Penrith. Passenger services on this beautifully scenic route ceased during 1972. *(RL Sewell)*

Saturday 19th March 1966. Seen here near Oxenholme, a Fairburn version of the class 4 2-6-4 tank, No 42095, is working hard at the rear of a heavy down goods train being hauled by a Black 5. This was one of the few Brighton-built examples constructed in 1951. She would be withdrawn from service during 1966. *(Carole Wilson)*

Sunday 2nd April 1966. This picturesque scene is at Cockermouth station showing the 9.25 Workington to Penrith and Carlisle service being operated by a 2-car Derby Lightweight DMU. Within three months of this photograph being taken, passenger services would cease to run on this section of line west of Keswick to Derwent Junction at Workington, and Cockermouth station would be closed. *(IS Carr)*

Sunday 2nd April 1966. Approaching Keswick station with a service from Workington to Penrith, this 2-car Derby Lightweight DMU has the high snow-covered fells as a spectacular backdrop. *(Derek Cross)*

Sunday 30th April 1966. Speeding south past the site of Grayrigg station is an unidentified Brush Type 4 at the head of a Perth to London Euston passenger train. This successful class of locomotive was to be increasingly seen working express passenger trains on both the East and West coast main lines. Sitting in the passing loop with a parcels train is Standard class 7P6F Britannia 4-6-2 No 70051 *Firth of Forth*. Constructed at Crewe works in 1954, she would be withdrawn at the end of 1967. *(MS Welch)*

Sunday 11th June 1966. This splendid panoramic photograph shows a 2-car Derby Lightweight DMU operating the 9.25 Carlisle to Whitehaven Bransty service, while in the background is the impressive industrial scene of the Moss Bay Iron and Steel works at Workington, famous for its production of rails. First manufactured here in 1877, production continued until 2006 when the plant closed. *(CT Gifford)*

Sunday 6th August 1966. Class 5 4-6-0 No 44675 speeds through the Lune Gorge with a southbound goods train. A 1950 Horwich-built example of this numerous class, she would be withdrawn in 1967. *(AR Thompson)*

Sunday 17th September 1966. This wonderfully moody photograph shows ex-LMS class 8F 2-8-0 No 48731 working north with a heavy goods train near Grayrigg. Built at Darlington works in 1945 as part of an order for the LNER, she became LMS property in 1946, and would survive until withdrawn in 1967. *(REB Siviter)*

Tuesday 19th September 1966. Ivatt-designed class 4 2-6-0 No 43006 is shuffling the 10.15 goods train from Moor Row at Rowrah station. The passenger services on this former Whitehaven, Cleator and Egremont Railway route had been withdrawn as early as April 1931, but goods services continued until 1978. The Mogul was constructed at Horwich works in 1948, and would be withdrawn after 20 years' service in 1968. The owner of the washing on the station fence must have been annoyed about the timing of this trains arrival. *(HB Oldroyd)*

Tuesday 28th November 1966. Skirting the edge of Morecambe Bay, and with a glimpse of Grange-over-Sands station in the background, ex-LMS class 5 4-6-0 No 45226 accelerates toward Barrow with a parcels train. Built in 1936 by Armstrong Whitworth, she would be withdrawn in 1967. *(RE Ruffell)*

Tuesday 28th February 1967. With Oxenholme station and locomotive depot in the background, a 2-car Derby Lightweight DMU operates a Carnforth to Windermere service. Opened in 1847, the Windermere branch would be reduced to a single track in 1972/3. *(CT Gifford)*

Saturday 1st April 1967. Brush Type 4 No D1855 is about the breast the summit at Shap with a northbound goods train. This efficient, hardworking and reliable class of locomotives was so successful that over 500 examples were built, and their use continued well into the 21st century. This example was built in 1965 at Crewe; it would be numbered 47205 in the TOPS scheme and later renumbered 47395 before being withdrawn in 2001. It was purchased for preservation and is currently based at the Northampton and Lamport Railway. *(Derek Cross)*

Friday 26th May 1967. Easing its speed for the 70mph restriction at Wreay, just south of Carlisle, Brush Type 4 No D1857 is heading north with the down Royal Scot consisting of 12 coaches. Built at Crewe works in 1965, this locomotive would be withdrawn in 2001 numbered 47207. *(JL McIvor)*

Friday 26th May 1967. Heading south at Wreay near Carlisle, Brush Type 4 No D1620 is working the 11.20 Perth to Birmingham passenger train. Another Crewe works example, built in 1964, it would be numbered 47039 in the TOPS scheme and later re-numbered 47565 before being withdrawn in 2000. *(JL McIvor)*

July 1967. Heading a train of Freightliner containers from Glasgow to London through the beautifully misty scenery of the River Lune valley near Tebay is Brush Type 4 No D1808. Constructed by Brush at its Loughborough works in 1965, it would be withdrawn in 1992 numbered 47327. *(JH Cooper-Smith)*

Friday 21st July 1967. Standard class 7P6F Britannia 4-6-2 No 70049 *Solway Firth*, here minus nameplates, is working a 15-coach train of empty stock from Morecambe to Glasgow just north of the former station at Grayrigg. As members of this class of locomotive were replaced by diesels in other regions, the remaining examples finished their working lives on the northern stretches of the LMR. This example was constructed at Crewe works in 1954, and would be withdrawn at the end of 1967. *(JH Cooper-Smith)*

Saturday 22nd July 1967. With a full head of steam, Standard class 7P6F Britannia 4-6-2 No 70038 *Robin Hood* is working the 14.00 Saturdays-only Glasgow to Liverpool express at Thrimby Grange south of Penrith. This locomotive was built at Crewe works in 1954, and would be withdrawn in August 1967. *(David E Gouldthorp)*

Saturday 23rd July 1967. Brush Type 4 No D1857 has just passed Dent signalbox, seen in the background, with the 11.10 Birmingham to Glasgow train diverted due to engineering works on the WCML. *(JH Cooper-Smith)*

Saturday 5th August 1967. This fine photograph shows the track layout at the southern end of Hest Bank station with Standard class 4 4-6-0 No 75015 waiting in the Morecambe branch while ex-LMS class 5, 4-6-0 No 44971 moves light engine on the up main line. Just beyond the short station platforms, water can be seen glistening in the up water trough. 75015 was a Swindon works product of 1951 destined to be withdrawn at the end of 1967, while the Black 5 was built at Crewe works in 1946, and would be withdrawn in August 1968. *(Eric Doel)*

Saturday 5th August 1967. Another view from the Morecambe branch at Hest Bank with a surprised looking driver of ex-LMS class 8F 2-8-0 No 48664 getting the right of way to proceed onto the main line. Constructed in 1944 at Brighton works as part of an order for the Railway Executive, she would survive to be withdrawn in October 1967. *(Eric Doel)*

Friday 2nd February 1968. At Carnforth depot with a background of "dead" steam locomotives, BR/Sulzer Type 2 No D5207 moves slowly in the yard. Constructed in 1963 at Derby works, it would be withdrawn in 1987 numbered 25057 in the TOPS scheme and sold to a private buyer. It is currently based at the North Norfolk Railway. *(NE Preedy)*

Sunday 17th March 1968. The last working Britannia, No 70013 *Oliver Cromwell*, is seen here departing Carnforth with a special. Destined to survive into preservation, she was constructed at Crewe works in 1951 and withdrawn from British Railways service after her last duty on 11th August 1968. She is now part of the National Collection, and is based with the Great Central Railway at Loughborough. *(WS Sellar)*

Monday 29th April 1968. Introduced in 1967 to handle traffic on the WCML north of Crewe, prior to the completion of the electrification work to Glasgow, the 50 examples of the later English Electric built Type 4s were powerful locomotives. Seen here working north with an express at Hest Bank water troughs is No D414. Built in 1968 at the Vulcan Foundry, she was later numbered 50014 and named *Warspite* before being withdrawn in 1987. *(TW Nicholls)*

Monday 29th April 1968. English Electric Type 4 No D415 is heading the up Royal Scot as it speeds through Carnforth. Constructed at the Vulcan Foundry in 1968, it would be renumbered 50015 in the TOPS scheme and subsequently named *Valiant*. The locomotive would be withdrawn in 1992, and is currently based at the East Lancashire Railway awaiting restoration. *(TW Nicholls)*

Tuesday 30th April 1968. English Electric Type 4 No D407 is working an up express over Hest Bank troughs. Built in 1968 at the Vulcan Foundry, it would later be numbered 50007 and named *Hercules*. Withdrawn from service in 1994, it would be bought privately and is currently based at the Midland Railway Centre, painted green and named *Sir Edward Elgar*. *(TW Nicholls)*

Saturday 4th May 1968. Ex-LMS class 5 4-6-0 No 45095 is showing severe signs of leaking glands but is still making good headway with a class 9 goods working southbound near Lancaster. The shed code (10A) indicates that she is allocated to Springs Branch depot. Built at the Vulcan Foundry in 1935, she would survive until the last days of main line steam traction on British Railways, being withdrawn during August 1968.
(Eric Doel)

Saturday 15th June 1968. Metropolitan-Vickers Type 2 No D5712 heads over the former site of Dillicar water troughs with a down ballast train for Carlisle. Built in 1959, it would survive a further three months after this photograph was taken before being withdrawn, having given only nine years of service. *(David Wharton)*

Saturday 13th July 1968. One of the few remaining Black 5s No 44874 is seen here approaching Oxenholme with the 12.25 Windermere to Carnforth local while deputising for a failed DMU. Built at Crewe works in 1945, she would be withdrawn at the end of main line steam operations on British Railways in August 1968. *(JB Mounsey)*

Sunday 11th August 1968. This momentous day sees English Electric Type 4 No D244 approaching Ais Gill with the 11.50 Glasgow to Manchester express. Diverted from the WCML due to other events taking place, the locomotive was built at the Vulcan Foundry in 1959, and would be withdrawn in 1985 numbered 40044. *(David Wharton)*

Sunday 11th August 1968. Journey's end – the Manchester Victoria to Blackburn and Carlisle leg of the Fifteen Guinea Special has arrived at Carlisle behind Standard class 7P6F Britannia 4-6-2 No 70013 *Oliver Cromwell*. The locomotive's next appearance would be at Alan Bloom's Bressingham Steam Museum where she resided for many years. She had initially been allocated to East Anglian depots for over ten years before being moved to the LMR and ending her service based at Carnforth depot. *(IS Carr)*